The Story of—
Through the Roof!

As Told in Luke 5:17-26
(New Revised Standard Version)

One day, while [Jesus] was teaching, Pharisees and teachers of the law were sitting near by (they had come from every village of Galilee and Judea and from Jerusalem); and the power of the Lord was with him to heal. Just then some men came, carrying a paralyzed man on a bed. They were trying to bring him in and lay him before Jesus; but finding no way to bring him in because of the crowd, they went up on the roof and let him down with his bed through the tiles into the middle of the crowd in front of Jesus. When he saw their faith, he said, "Friend, your sins are forgiven you." Then the scribes and the Pharisees began to question, "Who is this who is speaking blasphemies? Who can forgive sins but God alone?" When Jesus perceived their questionings, he answered them, "Why do you raise such questions in your hearts?

Which is easier, to say, 'Your sins are forgiven you,' or to say 'Stand up and walk'? But so that you may know that the Son of Man has authority on earth to forgive sins"—he said to the one who was paralyzed—"I say to you, stand up and take your bed and go to your home." Immediately he stood up before them, took what he had been lying on, and went to his home, glorifying God. Amazement seized all of them, and they glorified God and were filled with awe, saying, "We have seen strange things today."

Production and Presentation Notes

Through the Roof! *brings together three complementary elements— music, drama, and worship—to create an exciting Christian education experience for children in grades 2 through 5.*

Music, as a vehicle by which language and stories of faith are passed on, has few equals. Drama allows children to move beyond the limits of personal experience, exploring and expressing the thoughts and feelings of biblical figures, and learning more about their own thoughts and feelings.

> *...their presentation, rather than being a performance or entertainment, is a gift to the congregation...*

This use of music and drama in worship reflects a growing appreciation for the educational function of congregational worship. Children involved in this musical receive practical experience in leading worship. They discover that their presentation, rather than being a performance or entertainment, is a gift to the congregation—a sharing of the

children's encounter with a wonderful story of friendship, faith, forgiveness, and healing.

The Cast

Through the Roof! is Terry Kirkland's joyful, inviting retelling of the Luke 5:17-26 account of a paralyzed man who was forgiven and healed by Jesus after being lowered through the roof by four friends. The story is introduced by two Greeters; told by the Homeowner, two Storytellers, a Scribe, and a Pharisee; and pantomimed by Jesus, the Four Friends, the Paralyzed Man, and the people in the crowd. The entire cast sings all of the songs. The presentation takes approximately 20 minutes.

Assign the seven speaking parts to girls and boys with good stage presence, strong voices, and the ability to memorize, or who show potential in these areas. "Holding Auditions," on page 40, will guide you in auditioning persons for speaking and pantomimed roles.

> ## *The presentation takes approximately 20 minutes.*

The pantomimed roles call for expressive children who move well on stage. Creating the illusion of the man being lowered through the roof is the responsibility of those persons with pantomimed roles.

Children in the crowd will have an opportunity to create special characters for themselves.

If memorization is an obstacle, you have the option of allowing the speakers to read their lines from the pulpit or lectern with the aid of a microphone. Involve children who prefer not to sing by assigning them to speaking and pantomimed roles. These children can participate in the entire experience by working at the small group activities while the singers are learning the music.

The Set

Anticipation builds immediately as the congregation enters the sanctuary and sees the inside of the house where the story takes place. Four cardboard or foam core board figures—silhouettes of the children portraying the Homeowner, Jesus, the Scribe, and the Pharisee—are clothed in costumes identical to those worn by these four characters. As the characters are introduced, they enter, set their silhouettes aside, and stand where the silhouettes had originally been placed, thus bringing their characters to life.

Some churches will choose to have each of the children make a silhouette, creating the illusion of a crowd. The crowd silhouettes may be painted in biblical dress

or simply in a solid color. If you choose not to use the silhouettes, adapt by having the Homeowner, Jesus, the Scribe, and the Pharisee enter and take their places during the "Prelude and Greeting" music, before the Greeters speak.

Preparation and Presentation

Unique to *Through the Roof!* is the step-by-step preparation and presentation process that provides leaders with the tools needed to assist children in

- experiencing the story and relating it to contemporary life;
- learning the music;
- building the set;
- auditioning and rehearsing for the speaking and pantomimed roles;
- creating their individual characters;
- staging the drama;
- understanding their role as worship leaders;
- preparing publicity materials;
- selecting or assembling costumes.

As you begin organizing for your experience of this musical, schedule a meeting with your leadership team and persons responsible for planning congregational worship. Clear the necessary preparation and presentation time on the church calendar for *Through the Roof!* and designate the worship service when it will be presented. Structure the service so that the musical serves as a proclamation of the Word.

Unique to Through the Roof! is the step-by-step preparation and presentation process

In each session, the "Preparation" section lets leaders know what materials they will need and what they will need to do to go into the session ready to lead. The "Into the Story" section allows the children to experience the biblical

account in many ways, always beginning with activities designed to accommodate children who arrive early. "Into the Songs" gives complete plans for teaching the music. The "Small Group Activities" section involves the children in production-related activities. "Closing" brings the group back together again for closing devotions. In Sessions 7–10, "Into the Service" replaces "Into the Story" and prepares the children for the worship experience.

Schedules and Adaptations

Following the suggested plan, schedule sessions over the course of 8 or 9 weeks, with Session 9 (dress rehearsal) taking place the day before the presentation. Plan ninety-minute blocks of time for Sessions 1 through 8 and a two-hour block for Session 9, the dress rehearsal. Designating the presentation as Session 10 affirms the presentation as part of the total learning experience.

> ### *Plan ninety-minute blocks of time for Sessions 1 through 8 and a two-hour block for Session 9, the dress rehearsal.*

If church schedules cannot accommodate sessions of the suggested length, extend the preparation over additional weeks or eliminate some of the learning experiences. Consider the time available, the number of children, the age range and musical ability of the children, and adapt as your situation requires.

If you choose to condense the process into five longer sessions, combine Sessions 1 and 2, 3 and 4, 5 and 6, and 7 and 8. Using this option, move from "Into the Story" and "Into the Songs" in the first of the combined sessions to the same categories in the second. Combine small group activities from both sessions, add a break/snack time, and use closing devotions from the second session. Make similar adaptations for one week choral camps, day camps, or vacation Bible schools.

If your church has a small number of children, consider using *Through the Roof!* as an

---

Through the Roof! Components

LEADER/ACCOMPANIST EDITION (Item Code No. 419115). Copies needed for persons leading the learning activities, teaching the music, and providing piano accompaniment.

Singer's Edition (Item Code No. 41914X). Contains the biblical account, music (lyrics and melody line), narration and stage directions, learning activities, and an autograph page. One copy needed for each singer and leader.

Listening Tape (Item Code No. 419123). One copy needed for the group. Contains the complete musical with narration, songs, and full instrumentation. Purchase additional copies for children to use for rehearsing between sessions and to enjoy at home—especially as a reminder of their experience with *Through the Roof!*

Instrumental Recording (Item Code No. 419131). One copy needed for the group. Contains accompaniment only; full instrumentation—keyboard, acoustic guitar, bass guitar, strings, trumpet, flute, piccolo, oboe, clarinet, soprano saxophone, English horn, and percussion.

intergenerational experience. Adults and youth will find themselves captivated by the lovely music and lively narration. Adapted to allow all ages to learn together, the session plans offer guidance for a powerful experience of cross-generational education.

Leadership Needed

Leadership for *Through the Roof!* will be most effectively managed by two primary leaders—one concentrating on learning activities related to the story, and another concentrating on teaching the music. Recruit other leaders as necessary to coordinate the small group activities:

• assisting the children in creating the set and silhouettes (see pages 36–39);

• coordinating auditions (page 40), line rehearsals (page 41), and staging (43);

• working with bulletin covers (see Sessions 5 and 6) and publicity (page 42); and

• making or assigning costumes (pages 44–45).

Permission to duplicate pages 36–45, containing instructions for small group activities, is granted with the purchase of this LEADER/ACCOMPANIST EDITION. Have leaders recruit additional helpers as needed.

Permission to duplicate pages 36–45, containing instructions for small group activities, is granted with the purchase of this LEADER/ACCOMPANIST EDITION.

With the division of leadership responsibilities among several adults or older youth, anticipate a delightfully stress-free experience for leaders *and* children!

Materials Needed

❑ assortment of bulletins from typical Sunday worship services

❑ assortment of magazines with colorful illustrations or photographs

❑ Bibles (*New Revised Standard Version*)

❑ blindfolds, one for every two children

❑ cassette player

❑ clear tape

❑ colored felt-tip markers

❑ construction paper

❑ crayons

❑ gummed stars

❑ large sheets of paper

❑ magazine pictures of crowds of people

❑ masking tape

❑ materials for "Building the Set" (see pages 36–37)

❑ materials for "Costuming the Cast" (see pages 44–45)

❑ materials for "Creating the Silhouettes" (see pages 38–39)

❑ materials for "Preparing Publicity" (see page 42)

❑ milk

❑ name tags

❑ pencils

❑ photocopies of the audition guide (see page 40)

❑ piano

❑ slices of orange or lemon

❑ three small glasses

❑ white glue

❑ white paper

Session One

Preparation

Materials
- name tags
- gummed stars
- masking tape
- assortment of magazines with colorful illustrations or photographs
- large sheets of paper
- white glue or clear tape
- felt-tip marker
- cassette player
- materials for "Building the Set" (see page 36)

Make Name Tags/Attendance Keepers

Make name tags for all participants—singers, leaders, and helpers. Print *Through the Roof!* on the top of the name tags and leave a space in the middle for names to be written in large letters. Learn all children's names and encourage other leaders to do the same.

Leave space on the bottom of the name tags for session numbers or gummed stars to indicate the sessions attended.

Prepare the Songs to Learn Poster

Prepare the Songs to Learn poster as illustrated. Mount the poster on the wall at the singers' eye level.

Through the Roof!
Songs to Learn

_____ 1. "Hello, My Good Neighbor"
_____ 2. "A Friend Is a Wonderful Thing"
_____ 3. "Faith"
_____ 4. "Praise to the Lord" (Short Version)
_____ 5. "Praise to the Lord" (Long Version)

Green check: music in hand
Brown check: sung with word clues
Blue check: memorized
Red check: ready for presentation

Collect Materials for the Good Neighbor Montage

Collect an assortment of magazines with colorful illustrations or photographs, a large sheet of paper, several containers of white glue or rolls of clear tape, and a felt-tip marker. Write "Hello, My Good Neighbor" in large letters on the paper, allowing space for magazine pictures that suggest what it means to be a good neighbor.

Have Materials Ready for the Back Wall of the House

See "Building the Set," on pages 36–37, and prepare materials for the children to begin painting the back wall of the house.

Review the Teaching Plan for Session One

Give special attention to the directions for teaching "Hello, My Good Neighbor" and "A Friend Is a Wonderful Thing."

Into the Story

Welcome the Children

Have the recording of *Through the Roof!* playing quietly as you welcome the children. Ask them to write their names on a name tag. Write a 1 for Session One or place a gummed star in the attendance space. Attach name tags with masking tape.

Begin the Good Neighbor Montage

Invite those who arrive early to look through the magazines and tear out pictures that show people being good neighbors. Have them glue or tape the pictures to the large sheet of paper headed "Hello, My Good Neighbor." Indicate that there will be time to continue work on the montage during the small group activities later on in the session.

Introduce the Story

Distribute copies of the *Through the Roof! Singer's Edition* and have the children write their names on the back cover. Then ask the children what stories of Jesus healing people they remember from the Bible. List the stories on a large sheet of paper. If the Luke 5:17-26 story of Jesus healing the paralyzed man isn't mentioned, add it to their list. Explain to younger children that "paralyzed" refers to a person—or a part of a person's body—that is unable to move. Tell them to follow along on page 1 in their books as you read the story. (If copies of the *New Revised Standard Version* are available, you may want the children to read directly from the Bible.) Encourage them to listen for new words. If you have older children who are confident readers, ask one or more of them to read.

Discuss New Words

Create a list of new words or words the children might have heard but can't define. Write the words on a large sheet of paper and give the children an opportunity to supply definitions. Their list might include:

Retell the Story

Divide the children into small groups of four or five, with different ages represented in each group. Have the small groups sit in circles. Ask the children to retell the story in their small groups, going from person to person with each one contributing details until the story is told. Start the process by retelling verse one in your own words, and then let the small groups continue.

When the small groups are done retelling the story, read the Luke 5:17-26 account to them once again.

Pharisees: A group of Jewish people who knew and strictly obeyed all Jewish religious laws

scribes: Jewish teachers of religious laws

Galilee: northern Israel—around the Sea of Galilee

Judea: southern Israel

Jerusalem: the city that is the religious and political center of Israel

paralyzed: unable to move all or a portion of one's body

sins: things we do or fail to do that cause problems for us with God, other people, and creation

blasphemies: things said against God or suggesting a person capable of something only God can do

forgive: not holding persons' mistakes against them

Son of Man: a title for Jesus that means he is human like us as well as being like God

glorify: to show in our words and actions that God is wonderful and does wonderful things

amazement: having trouble believing something that has happened

awe: being really impressed with something that has happened

Into the Songs

Introduce "Hello, My Good Neighbor"

Ask the children to imagine the great crowd gathering to see Jesus. Tell them that the first song they'll be learning, "Hello, My Good Neighbor," is the one that the people sing as the crowd gathers at the beginning of the story. Direct them to the song on page 4 in their books. Point out the first ending and repeat sign (♩) at the end of section A. Make sure they understand that they will hear section A twice before going ahead to the second ending and section B.

Ask the children to follow the words with their index fingers as you play the recording and to be ready to describe what they hear. As they listen, move through the group and make sure they are following their music correctly. Help those who are having difficulty.

After they have listened to the entire song, ask if they would like to point out anything particular that they noticed about the music. Call their attention to the I and II markings and ask if they heard two groups singing back and forth to each other. Tell them that they will be dividing into groups to sing the song that

way, but you want them to learn the entire song first.

Play through section A on the piano (or use the instrumental recording), then have the children sing it several times in unison (without dividing into groups I and II) until they can sing it with confidence.

Explain the Songs to Learn Poster

Point out the Songs to Learn poster and the names of the songs the children will be learning to help tell the story of *Through the Roof!* to the congregation. Tell the children that you will keep track of their progress by putting check marks on the lines before each title as the songs are learned. A green check will indicate that they can sing the song with music in hand; brown—that they can sing the song from word clues (pages 14-15 in the *Singer's Edition*); blue—that they can sing the song from memory; and red—that the song is ready for presentation to the congregation.

Introduce "A Friend Is a Wonderful Thing"

Point out the second song on the list, "A Friend Is a Wonderful Thing." Ask where in

the story they see an example of people showing friendship. (the four men bringing the paralyzed man to Jesus)

Have the children turn to "A Friend Is a Wonderful Thing," on page 6 in their books, and tell them to look through the song for the repeat sign, the first and second endings, and the sections labeled A and B.

Play the recording of the song and have the children follow the words with their fingers as they listen. Play the recording again and ask the children to listen carefully and be ready to tell you how many different melodies they hear. To encourage them to think and respond, accept all responses, but help them discover the two different melodies: A and B.

Have the children sing section A on a nonsense word such as "loo" or "beep," then have them slowly speak stanzas one and two in rhythm. When familiar with the melody and the lyrics, have them sing both stanzas of section A.

Thank the children for their good singing and for their excellent start on learning the first two songs.

Small Group Activities

Finish the Good Neighbor Montage

Allow the children to complete the Good Neighbor Montage. Suggest that they might want to

use the montage to decorate their room for now, and use it later as a poster to announce *Through the Roof!* to the congregation.

Begin Painting the Wall of the House

See the instructions for set construction on pages 36–37. Have the children begin work on the set by painting the wall of the house.

Closing

Bring the Children Together for a Closing

Call the children together and thank them for coming. Tell them that it is important for them to attend all rehearsals. Have them sing section A of "A Friend Is a Wonderful Thing." Lead them in the following prayer:

Thank you, God, for Bible stories. Thank you for time to explore the stories, for minds to remember them, for voices and bodies to tell them, and for music to sing them. Thank you for neighbors and friends who listen to our stories and enjoy them with us. We pray these words of thanks in Jesus' name. Amen.

Collect Name Tags

Collect the name tags and use them to create a list of participants and your own attendance record.

Notes

Session Two

Preparation

Materials
- [ ] name tags
- [ ] gummed stars
- [ ] masking tape
- [ ] two large sheets of paper
- [ ] blindfolds, one for every two children
- [ ] large paper for poster
- [ ] cassette player
- [ ] materials for "Building the Set" and "Creating the Silhouettes" (pages 36–39)

Create an Audition Schedule

Prepare a schedule for children to audition for the speaking and pantomimed roles. The persons conducting auditions should plan to spend three to five minutes with each child. Read "Holding Auditions," on page 40, and be prepared to lead well-organized, objective tryouts.

Prepare Sheets for Listing Activity

Secure two large sheets of paper. On one write "Things That Hinder," and on the other write "Things That Help." Tape the paper on walls at a level easily accessible to the children.

Invite a Guest to Talk About Handicapping Conditions

Unless you have an extended rehearsal period, you will want to choose either this or the trust walk activity. For this activity you will need to invite a person with a handicapping condition who would be willing to talk with the children about that condition. If possible, recruit someone whose handicap restricts mobility so that the children can begin to identify with the paralyzed man in the story. Be sure that your guest is clear about what he or she is expected to share with the children (see instructions for activity on page 11) and the length of time (no more than 10 minutes) designated for this activity.

Secure Blindfolds for a Trust Walk

If you opt for the trust walk rather than the guest, secure blindfolds—one for every two children. Decide on the area the children will be permitted to use for the trust walk.

Create a Faith Poster

On a large sheet of paper write the following verse based on the King James Version: "For faith is the substance of things hoped for, the evidence of things not seen." (Hebrews 11:1)

Have Materials Ready for the House and Silhouettes

Read "Building the Set" (pages 36–37) and "Creating the Silhouettes" (pages 38–39), and secure necessary materials for these two small group activities.

Review the Teaching Plan for Session Two

Give special attention to the directions for teaching "Faith."

Into the Story

Welcome the Children

Play the recording of "Hello, My Good Neighbor" as the children begin arriving. Greet them, record their attendance by placing a 2 or a gummed star on their name tags, and have them put their name tags on. Tell them that they may do either or both of the next two activities.

Schedule Auditions for Spoken and Pantomimed Roles

Invite the children to sign up to audition for the seven spoken roles and the six pantomimed roles. See "Holding Auditions," on page 40.

Create Lists Related to Handicapping Conditions

Ask the children to begin creating two lists on the large sheets of paper labeled "Things That Hinder" and "Things That Help." Under "Things That Hinder" have them list all of the handicapping conditions they can think of and the things that get in the way of persons with handicapping conditions. Under "Things That Help" they are to list the things that help these persons cope with things that get in the way (wheelchairs, crutches, walkers, elevators, buses and vans equipped with wheelchair lifts,

ramps, reading material printed in large type and in Braille, signing, seeing eye and hearing ear dogs, books on cassette tape, and so forth).

Sing "Hello, My Good Neighbor"

To bring the group together, begin singing "Hello, My Good Neighbor" and have the children sing along as they take their seats.

Explore the Paralyzed Man's Perspective

Ask the children to think of people they know who have handicapping conditions. Let the children suggest other things that help or hinder. Add these suggestions to the lists.

Ask them to tell which of the Things That Hinder were problems for people in Bible times, and which of the Things That Help were available to those people. Circle the items mentioned. Point out that we have many more ways to deal today with handicapping conditions. Read Luke 5:17-26 once again and have the children follow along in their books, listening carefully for those parts that tell about the paralyzed man.

Discuss Handicapping Conditions With a Guest
(Option 1)

Have your guest talk with the children about his or her handicapping condition and the special challenges that it presents. Encourage your guest to focus on how this condition has influenced his or her trusting relationships with other people—especially family and friends. Since the Luke 5:17-26 account focuses on healing, the question as to why some people are healed and others are not may come up. You or your guest will want to speak to the mystery of healing—something beyond our ability to understand.

Go on a Trust Walk
(Option 2)

Arrange the children in pairs and have them take turns blindfolding and leading their partners on a short trust walk—no longer than three minutes. Give them specific boundaries for the walk and remind them that they are responsible for their partner's safety. After the trust walks are completed, lead a brief discussion helping the children focus on their feelings about having to depend on another person or having another person depend on them.

Into the Songs

Continue Learning "Hello, My Good Neighbor"

Tell the children to find "Hello, My Good Neighbor," on page 4. Play the recording again and ask the children to sing section A, which they learned last session, and just listen to the rest of the song. Ask if they heard another part of the song that sounded like section A. (Section C is exactly the same but with different words.)

Play the recording again. Have the children sing sections A and C and just listen to the rest of the song. Ask them which parts of the song they haven't learned. (sections B and D) Teach section B, paying particular attention to the crescendo, ritard, and fermata on the phrase, "Oh what a day, we are all on our way to see Jesus." Practice it several times until everyone is able to get louder, slow down, and to hold and release the second syllable of "Jesus" together. Sing again the parts of the song they know.

Continue Learning "A Friend Is a Wonderful Thing"

Tell the children to turn to "A Friend Is a Wonderful Thing," on page 6, and have them sing along with the recording. Have them sing the two stanzas of section A that they know, and just listen to the rest of the song. Ask them to tell you which parts of the song they do not know (section B and the second ending), then teach section B.

Introduce "Faith"

Ask the children to recall where the word "faith" appears in the story of the paralyzed man. Allow time for them to respond, and then read Luke 5:20. "When he [Jesus] saw their faith, he said, 'Friend, your sins are forgiven you.'" Ask whose faith Jesus was talking about (the ones who brought the paralyzed man to Jesus), and how these persons showed their faith (believing in Jesus enough to bring the paralyzed man for healing).

Ask the children to share their ideas about faith. Then, have a child read Hebrews 11:1 (King James Version) from the poster you have made: "For faith is the substance of things hoped for, the evidence of things not seen." Say the verse in the same rhythm that is used in the song and then have the children repeat it together two or three times in rhythm.

Tell the children to find the song on page 8. Play the recording and ask the children to watch and listen for the places in the music where they hear Hebrews 11:1. (sections C and F) After they have listened, teach that particular phrase and have them sing it from both places in the music.

Have the children tell you how section F differs from section C. (A final word, "faith," is added.) Teach the ending and have them sing these two sections. Keep the Faith poster on the wall for use in Session Four.

Small Group Activities

Continue Painting the House

After a base coat of a solid color has been applied to the wall of the house, have the children begin giving the wall a design that looks like rough clay bricks and stone. See "Building the Set," on pages 36–37.

Audition Persons for Speaking and Pantomimed Roles

Allow the children who did not have time to sign up for an audition to do so. See "Holding Auditions," on page 40, for suggestions as to how to organize this time.

Begin Work on the Silhouettes

Ask the children to work in pairs. One child will lie down on a cardboard or foam core board while his or her partner traces around his or her body. Encourage the children to come up with creative positions. Once the basic shapes have been outlined, have the children begin to sketch in details to their silhouettes—physical features and biblical costume. See "Creating the Silhouettes," on pages 38–39, for additional instructions.

Closing

Bring the Children Together for a Closing

Call the children together and thank them for coming. Remind them of the importance of their attendance at each rehearsal. Ask them to sing section F of "Faith."

Say an Echo Prayer

Lead the children in the following prayer, having them echo each line after you:

> *For the faith that keeps us hoping,*
>
> *for the unseen things in which we believe;*
>
> *for the people we trust*
>
> *and the love we receive:*
>
> *we give you praise, O Lord!*
>
> *Amen!*

Collect Name Tags

Collect the name tags and update your attendance record.

Notes

Session Three

Preparation

Materials
❏ name tags
❏ gummed stars
❏ masking tape
❏ construction paper
❏ colored felt-tip markers
❏ large sheet of paper
❏ cassette player
❏ materials for "Building the Set" and "Creating the Silhouettes" (pages 36–39)

Prepare for Auditions

Review your notes from the previous session's auditions. Make a schedule for auditions to be held during this session.

Make a "A Friend Is a Wonderful Thing" Banner

Use several pieces of colored construction paper taped together horizontally to make a banner. With colored felt-tip markers, write "A Friend Is a Wonderful Thing" across the banner. Tape it to the wall in an area that will allow the children space to add pictures of friends and lists of characteristics of friends beneath the banner. Have paper, felt-tip markers and/or crayons ready for the children's pictures and lists.

Prepare a Sheet for the Word Web

In the center of a large sheet of paper, write the word "friends." Post the sheet in front of the room where it can be seen by the entire group and where you will be able to add words to the sheet during the session.

Have Materials Ready for the House and Silhouettes

Assemble the materials necessary to continue work on these two parts of the set. See pages 36–39.

Review the Teaching Plan for Session Three

Give special attention to the directions for teaching "Faith" and "Praise to the Lord" (Short Version), and for leading the discussion about friendship.

Into the Story

Welcome the Children

Play the recording of "A Friend Is a Wonderful Thing" as the children arrive. Greet them, place a 3 or a gummed star on their name tags, and have them put their name tags on.

Schedule Auditions for Spoken and Pantomimed Roles

Invite children interested in one of the spoken or pantomimed roles to sign up for an audition time. See "Holding Auditions," on page 40.

Focus on a Friend

As children arrive, ask each to either draw a picture of a friend or make a list of things that make a specific person his or her friend. Post drawings and lists under "A Friend Is a Wonderful Thing" banner.

Sing "A Friend Is a Wonderful Thing"

To bring the group together, have the children sing "A Friend Is a Wonderful Thing" as they take their seats.

Do a Word Web on Friends

Invite the children to suggest words and short phrases that they think of when they hear the word "friends." Write their suggestions on the large sheet of paper with the word "friends"

on it. If the words "trust," "helpful," or "dependable" are not mentioned, add them to the list. Use these words to assist the children in remembering the previous session's emphasis on trust. Draw lines between the words, creating a webbed effect, to represent the connections between the words.

Discuss How Friendship Is Shown in the Story

Tell the children to turn to the story on page 1 of their books. Ask them to watch and listen for the word "friend" as you or one of your confident readers reads the story, then lead them in discussion with the following questions:
Was the word "friend" used in the story? (yes)
Who was speaking at the time? (Jesus)
Who was being spoken to? (the paralyzed man)
Are the persons who brought the paralyzed man to Jesus ever referred to as friends? (no)
Why, do you think, do people who talk about this story call these men friends? What did they do to show friendship?

Into the Songs

Continue Learning "A Friend Is a Wonderful Thing"

Have the children find "A Friend Is a Wonderful Thing," on page 6, and look at the second ending. Ask them to describe what they see. (the same melody as the first ending except that there are two notes for the words, -ful thing, and a spoken Friends!) Teach the upper notes now and practice the spoken Friends!

Sing through the entire song, adding the ending you have just learned, and put a green check

mark on the Songs to Learn poster in front of "A Friend Is a Wonderful Thing."

Continue Learning "Faith"

Have the children find "Faith," on page 8. Tell them that the song is divided into sections which are lettered. Have them look through their music and tell you how many sections they can find. (six sections, A through F)

Remind the children that two of the sections are alike. Ask them to listen to the recording

and be ready to tell you if any of the other sections are repeated. Play the recording two or three times and have the children follow the music. Team up some of your better music readers with those less experienced so that all can follow along. They should remember that section C is like F with the final word "Faith" added as an ending, and discover that A is like D with a descant added and B is like E.

Teach sections A and B and then sing the parts of the song the children know.

Continue Learning "Hello, My Good Neighbor"

Have the children turn to "Hello, My Good Neighbor," on page 4, and review the parts of the song they know. Then have them find section D and describe what happens there. ("Oh, what a great day" is repeated softer and slower.) Practice section D.

Sing the entire song with the music and then put a green check mark on the Songs to Learn poster.

Introduce "Praise to the Lord" (Short Version)

Congratulate the children on having earned two green check marks and then have them find "Praise to the Lord" (Short Version), on page 11. Ask them to tell you how many sections this song has. (three—A, B, and C)

Play section A of the recording and have the children follow their music. Teach that section.

Ask the children to follow the words with their fingers as you

play the recording again. Instruct them to be ready to tell you how section B is like section A. (It begins the same but has a different ending.) Teach section B, calling attention to the dotted lines connecting sections A and B at the words *strings* and *O*. Explain that the dotted lines mean to continue singing without taking a breath. Practice that a few times, then sing both sections.

Small Group Activities

Continue Painting the House

Continue working on the clay brick and stone pattern of the back wall of the house. See "Building the Set," on pages 36–37.

Audition Persons for Speaking and Pantomimed Roles

Allow children who have not signed up for an audition to do so. Strive to complete auditions (see "Holding Auditions," on page 40) during this session so that selections can be announced and line rehearsals can begin next session.

Continue Work on the Silhouettes

Continue the work begun on the silhouettes in the previous session. Those who have not started their silhouettes should do so. Those who have started theirs should cut them out and begin painting in the details. See "Creating the Silhouettes," on pages 38–39.

Closing

Bring the Children Together for a Closing

Call the children together and thank them for coming. Sing sections A and B of "Praise to the Lord" (Short Version) as a closing song.

Create a Litany of Praise

Create a litany of praise by inviting the children to mention wonderful things the Lord has done. Use section B of "Praise to the Lord" (Short Version) as a response to their statements.

Collect Name Tags

Collect the name tags and update your attendance record.

Notes

Session Four

Preparation

Materials
- [ ] name tags
- [ ] gummed stars
- [ ] masking tape
- [ ] large sheets of paper
- [ ] colored felt-tip markers
- [ ] cassette player
- [ ] Faith poster from Session 2

Prepare the Graffiti Wall

Cover a large section of a wall with large sheets of paper.

Grocery bags cut and opened up will work well. Use colored markers to write "Jesus" in large letters on the paper—like you might find on a wall of graffiti. Have felt-tip markers ready for the children to use.

Select Persons for Spoken and Pantomimed Roles

Use the audition forms to guide you in selecting which of the children will be assigned the spoken and pantomimed roles. Make a list to post for the children to see after the characters have been announced.

Review the Teaching Plan for Session Four

Give special attention to the discussion of the meaning of faith. Make sure that the Faith poster from Session 2 is still on the wall.

Into the Story

Welcome the Children

Play the recording of "Praise to the Lord" (Short Version) as the children begin arriving. Greet them, record their attendance by placing a 4 or a gummed star on their name tags, and have them put their name tags on.

Create a Graffiti Wall

Invite the children to write things that they know about Jesus on the graffiti wall. Their graffiti messages could be names or symbols for Jesus, sayings of Jesus, or statements about things Jesus did.

Sing "Praise to the Lord" (Short Version)

To bring the group together, have the children sing sections A and B of "Praise to the Lord" (Short Version) as they take their seats.

Explore the Role of Jesus in the Story

Direct the children's attention to the graffiti wall. Affirm what the children already know about Jesus. Emphasize learnings from the previous three sessions.

Ask the children to follow along in their books as you read the story and to find and underline the first three things the story tells about Jesus. (He was teaching, the power of the Lord was with him to heal, he saw faith in the persons who brought the paralyzed man.)

Discuss the Meaning of Faith

Direct the children's attention to the Hebrews 11:1 definition of faith on the Faith poster from Session Two. Have them turn in their books to section C on page 9 and read those same words there. Invite the children who wish to do so to share some of the things they are hoping for. Expect anything from getting a new bike to world peace. Ask them what will fill the time between now and when what they hope for happens.

Explain that substance is the stuff that things are made of. Give an example such as what chairs are made of. To say that faith is the substance of the things we hope for is to say that faith is the stuff that hope is made of. Faith fills the time between now and when what we're hoping for happens. Faith is a gift from God—the gift of a picture in our minds of what we hope will happen. This picture reminds us that it *can* happen and calls us to do whatever we can to make sure it *does* happen.

Ask the children: "When people come into this room when none of you are here, what evidence would they find that we have been working on *Through the Roof!* here?" (posters, drawings, music, and so forth) Tell them that faith is evidence too—evidence that what we hope for is possible, even though we don't see it yet.

Have the children repeat the definition of faith in section C, speaking the words in rhythm.

Into the Songs

Continue Learning "Faith"

Have the children turn to page 8, sing section A of "Faith," and listen to section B. Next, teach section B and have the children sing it from section B and E in their music.

Tell the children to sing along on all the parts of the song they know, and just listen to the other parts as you play the recording again. Ask them to tell you which parts they will not sing. (the descant of section D) Sing the entire song, omitting only the descant. If you will not be using the descant, place a green check mark on the Songs to Learn poster in front of "Faith." If you will be using the descant, wait until it has been learned before adding the check mark.

Continue Learning "Praise to the Lord" (Short Version)

Have the children find "Praise to the Lord" (Short Version), on page 11. Have them sing sections A and B and listen to C.

Teach section C and then have the children sing the entire song. Put a green check mark on the Songs to Learn poster in front of "Praise to the Lord" (Short Version).

Continue Learning "Hello, My Good Neighbor"

Have the children turn to page 4 and sing "Hello, My Good Neighbor" from their music. Explain that the next step in learning this song is to be able to sing it without looking at the music. Ask them to find the word clues, on page 14. Ask them to examine the clues and tell you what they see. (the beginnings of phrases and key words to help them remember what to sing about next) Talk through the words of the song, using the word clues as a guide, and then sing the song from the clues. Put a brown check mark on the Songs to Learn poster in front of "Hello, My Good Neighbor."

Continue Learning "A Friend Is a Wonderful Thing"

Ask the children to turn to "A Friend Is a Wonderful Thing," on page 6, and to sing it from their music. Ask them to find the word clues for this song on page 14. Point out the repeat sign. Have them sing the song from the word clues. After they sing, add a brown check mark to the Songs to Learn poster in front of "A Friend Is a Wonderful Thing."

Small Group Activities

Begin Line Rehearsals

Before the children disperse for small group activities, announce which children have been chosen for the speaking and pantomimed roles. Post a list of the children who will be taking these roles. Tell the children that everyone else will be creating their own characters and ask them to be thinking about what kind of person they would like to portray in the crowd.

Gather those with the speaking roles together and walk them through the script. Have each of them highlight his or her lines and stage directions with transparent colored markers as you read through all lines. Instruct the children to be rehearsing their lines at home. Send a note home to families to alert them to be assisting with line rehearsal at home.

Finish Painting the House

Finish painting the clay brick and stone design on the walls of the house. See "Building the Set," on pages 36–37.

Continue Work on the Silhouettes

Continue the work begun on the silhouettes in the previous sessions. Once the painting is completed, add the pieces to the backs of the silhouettes to make them stand upright. See "Creating the Silhouettes," on pages 38–39.

Closing

Bring the Children Together for a Closing

Call the children together and thank them for coming. Ask them to sing "A Friend Is a Wonderful Thing" from the word clues on page 14.

Say an Echo Prayer

Repeat the prayer from Session Two, having the children echo each line after you.

For the faith that keeps us hoping,

for the unseen things in which we believe;

for the people we trust

and the love we receive:

we give you praise, O Lord!

Amen!

Collect Name Tags

Collect the name tags and update your attendance record.

Notes

Session Five

Preparation

Materials
- ❑ name tags
- ❑ gummed stars
- ❑ construction paper
- ❑ masking tape
- ❑ felt-tip markers or crayons
- ❑ pencils
- ❑ large sheet of paper
- ❑ orange or lemon
- ❑ knife
- ❑ milk
- ❑ three small glasses
- ❑ three blindfolds
- ❑ materials for "Creating the Silhouettes"
- ❑ white paper
- ❑ black felt-tip markers, fine-point and broad-tip
- ❑ cassette player

Choose a Surprising Outfit
For this session, all leaders should wear something unexpected—something that will really surprise the children.

Make a "Surprise!" Banner
Make a construction paper banner that reads "Surprise!" Tape it to the wall where the children will be able to add pictures or written descriptions of surprises they have experienced. Have paper, felt-tip markers and/or crayons, and pencils ready.

Gather Materials for the Surprising Experiment
Gather an orange or a lemon, a knife to slice it into sections, some milk, two or three small glasses, and two or three blindfolds. At the top of a large sheet of paper, write "Recipe for a Surprise" and tape the paper to the wall where it can be seen by the group.

Gather Materials for Bulletin Cover Illustrations
Gather sheets of bulletin-sized white paper, pencils, and black felt-tip markers—some fine-point and some broad-tip.

Review the Teaching Plan for Session Five
Give special attention to the "Faith" descant, the motions for "A Friend Is a Wonderful Thing," and the rhythmic prayer for use during the closing.

Into the Story

Welcome the Children

Play the recording of "Faith" as the children begin arriving. Greet them, record their attendance by placing a 5 or a gummed star on their name tags, and have them put their name tags on. Respond to questions about your attire by asking: "What were you expecting me to wear today?"

Draw Pictures of Surprises

Have the children draw pictures or write paragraphs about times when something surprised them. Tape them up around the "Surprise!" banner.

Sing "Faith"

Have the children sing sections A, B, and C of "Faith" as they take their seats.

Conduct a Surprising Experiment

Ask for two or three volunteers to assist with an experiment. Ask volunteers if they have any food allergies, since some children are unable to have milk products. Blindfold the volunteers and hand each a small glass of milk. Do not tell them what is in the glass. Hold a fresh slice of lemon or orange under their noses while they drink what's in the glass. Remove the blindfolds and ask each volunteer about the experience. You'll find that expecting one thing and getting another can be a surprising thing. Thank the volunteers.

Ask: "What does it take to make a surprise?" List their responses on the sheet of paper titled "Recipe for a Surprise."

Discuss the Surprise of the Scribes and Pharisees

Explain that Pharisees were people who believed that strictly following all religious laws was how people demonstrated their faith in God. The scribes were teachers of the Law. To scribes and Pharisees, life was predictable: obey the laws and life is good; disobey the laws and life is bad.

Scribes and Pharisees believed only God could forgive sins. There was only one way for gaining God's forgiveness. Jesus surprised them by forgiving the sins of the paralyzed man without following that way.

Ask the children if any of the things on the "Recipe for a Surprise" list are in the story of the paralyzed man's healing.

Into the Songs

Continue Learning "Faith"

Ask the children to find "Faith," on page 8, and to look at section D. Have them sing the melody while you sing the descant. Ask them to sing softly and listen to both parts.

Ask a few children to sing the descant with you while everyone else sings the melody. Practice the two parts together, then sing the entire song. Put a green check mark on the Songs to Learn poster.

Continue Learning "Praise to the Lord" (Short Version)

Ask the children to find "Praise to the Lord" (Short Version) on page 11. After they have sung the entire song, have the children find the word clues on page 15. Talk through the clues and then have them sing the song from the word clues.

Put a brown check mark on the Songs to Learn poster in front of "Praise to the Lord" (Short Version).

Take the Next Step With "Faith"

Have the children sing "Faith" from their music to review the song. Then ask them to find the word clues on page 15. Talk through the clues and then have them sing "Faith" from the word clues. Put a brown check mark on the Songs to Learn poster.

Do Music and Motions to "A Friend Is a Wonderful Thing"

Have the children sing "A Friend Is a Wonderful Thing" from the word clues on page 14. Explain that they will be doing motions with this song and need to be able to sing the song from memory before learning the motions. Lead them in singing the song once again, without the music or word clues. Add a blue check mark to the Songs to Learn poster in front of "A Friend Is a Wonderful Thing" if they can sing it from memory. Show the movements for stanza one, speaking the lyrics as you demonstrate the motions.

- On *short*, bend your knees to appear short.
- On *tall*, stand up straight.
- On *any old size* make a circling motion with your arms and hands. Start with your arms together in front of your body. Circle them up over your head and out to either side, ending the motion with hands down at your sides on *at all*.
- Divide the group into four groups for the singing of *but a friend is a friend, is a friend, is a*

friend. On the first *friend*, group one puts their arms around the shoulders of the persons next to them. On the second *friend*, group two does the same, and so on from left to right across the stage. At the fermata on the fourth *friends*, everyone freezes into position with arms around shoulders.

• On *any time, any how, anywhere*, lower your arms and stand straight.

Continue Learning "Hello, My Good Neighbor"

Have the children sing "Hello, My Good Neighbor" from the word clues on page 14. Explain that they will be divided into two groups to enter the sanctuary while singing this song. Before they can practice their entrance, they need to have the song memorized. Sing the song from memory now and add a blue check mark to the Songs to Learn poster. Divide the children into groups I and II and practice singing back and forth in preparation for permanent group assignments later.

Small Group Activities

Begin Line Rehearsals

Rehearse with the **Greeters** together, with the **Scribe** and **Pharisee** together, and with **Homeowner** and the two **Storytellers** individually. Children with speaking roles should be able to read well and with dramatic emphasis. Next session, children memorizing their parts should be able to deliver their lines with limited prompting. (See "Rehearsing Lines," on page 41.)

Complete the Silhouettes

Finish painting the silhouettes and attaching the pieces to the back to make them stand upright. (See "Creating the Silhouettes," on pages 38–39.)

Create Worship Bulletin Cover Illustrations

Give the children bulletin-sized sheets of white paper. Ask them to draw pictures of the story of the paralyzed man for the worship bulletin to be used when *Through the Roof!* is presented. The children will need to do line drawings— lightly sketching with pencil and then using black markers to darken the lines. Have them write their names on the back of the paper. Next session, they will choose illustrations for the bulletins.

Closing

Bring the Children Together for a Closing

Call the children together and thank them for coming. Let the children choose which song they would like to sing for the closing.

Say a Rhythmic Prayer of Thanks

Begin patting your legs in a gentle rhythm. Ask the children to join in. Pray the following prayer, one line at a time, with the children echoing you:

Collect Name Tags

Collect the name tags and update your attendance record.

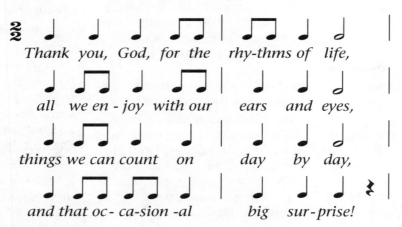

Thank you, God, for the rhy-thms of life,
all we en-joy with our ears and eyes,
things we can count on day by day,
and that oc-ca-sion-al big sur-prise!

Session Six

OVERVIEW

Preparation
Number Bulletin Illustrations
Prepare Crowd Pictures
Prepare for Staging Pantomimed
   Characters
Check Out Possibilities for Publicity
Prepare for Fitting the Children for
   Costumes
Review the Teaching Plan for Session Six

Into the Story
Welcome the Children
Choose Bulletin Illustration
Identify People in the Crowd
Sing "Praise to the Lord" (Short Version)
Develop Characters
Practice Characterizations

Into the Songs
Sing "Praise to the Lord" (Short Version)
   From Word Clues
Introduce "Praise to the Lord" (Long
   Version)
Do Music and Motions to "A Friend Is a
   Wonderful Thing"
Review "Hello, My Good Neighbor"
Continue Learning "Faith"

Small Group Activities
Conduct Line Rehearsals
Begin Staging Pantomimed Characters
Prepare Written Publicity Materials
Begin Fitting Children for Costumes

Closing
Bring the Children Together for a Closing
Collect Name Tags

Preparation

Materials
- ❑ name tags
- ❑ gummed stars
- ❑ masking tape
- ❑ bulletin illustrations
- ❑ small pieces of blank paper
- ❑ pencils
- ❑ magazine pictures of crowds of people
- ❑ tape/glue
- ❑ large piece of paper
- ❑ felt-tip markers
- ❑ house, table, step, and pallet for staging
- ❑ materials for "Costuming the Cast" (pages 44–45)
- ❑ cassette player

Number Bulletin Illustrations

Tape a number beside each of the bulletin illustrations so that children can choose their favorites by number. Have small blank pieces of paper and pencils for the children to make their selections.

Prepare Crowd Pictures

Select magazine pictures of crowds of people—one picture for every four or five children in your group. Tape or glue each of the pictures individually to the center of a large piece of paper. Tape the sheets on the wall at the children's eye level. Gather felt-tip markers for the activity.

Prepare for Staging Pantomimed Characters

Reserve the sanctuary for staging pantomimed characters. Set up the house if possible. Have the table, step, and pallet ready.

Check Out Possibilities for Publicity

Find out if the children can publicize *Through the Roof!* in the church newsletter or worship bulletins, how much space is available, and what deadlines they need to meet. Also see if the congregation would be open to having announcements by the children before or during Sunday school or worship. (See "Preparing Publicity," on page 42.)

Prepare for Fitting the Children for Costumes

See "Costuming the Cast," on pages 44–45, for guidance on creating or fitting costumes.

Review the Teaching Plan for Session Six

Give special attention to the activities for developing characters and practicing characterization.

Into the Story

Welcome the Children

Play the recording of "Praise to the Lord" (Short Version) as the children begin arriving. Greet them, record their attendance by placing a 6 or a gummed star on their name tags, and have them put their name tags on.

Choose Bulletin Illustration

Invite the children to select which illustration will be used for the worship bulletin cover when *Through the Roof!* is presented. Give each child a small blank piece of paper on which to write the number of the illustration he or she would like to see on the bulletin.

Identify People in the Crowd

Have each child circle a person who stands out in one of the crowd pictures. Tell the children to draw a line from the circle to a space on the paper around the picture, and to write at the other end of the line some words or phrases that describe why that person stands out.

Sing "Praise to the Lord" (Short Version)

To bring the group together, have the children sing "Praise to the Lord" (Short Version), as they take their seats.

Develop Characters

Ask the children: "What are some of the special things about you that make you stand out in a crowd of people?" Allow those children who wish to do so to respond. Remind the children that for the presentation of *Through the Roof!* some of them are taking the roles of specific persons—**Jesus**, the **Paralyzed Man**, the **Scribe**, and the **Pharisee.** We already know some reasons why these people might stand out in a crowd. But the other characters—the two **Greeters**, the **Homeowner**, the two **Storytellers**, the **Four Friends**, and all of the individuals in the crowd that gathered to hear Jesus—need to think about who they are and what makes them special. The **Homeowner** and the **Four Friends** need to be portrayed as adults, but all of the other characters can be any age they would like to be.

Invite the children to think about the characters they would like to portray in the story. Tell them to turn to page 16 in their books and follow along as you read the following questions:

• How old is your character?

• Is your character wealthy, poor, or in-between?

• Is your character outgoing or shy?

• What has your character heard about Jesus?

• Why was your character in the crowd? out of curiosity? because friends or family members were coming? to hear Jesus teach? to see Jesus heal people? to be forgiven or healed?

Have the children draw pictures of their characters or write descriptions of them. Encourage their creativity! Ask them to find partners and to tell one another about their characters. Suggest to the children that some of them might create a family unit or have their characters be friends.

Practice Characterizations

The children will need space for moving as they practice their characterizations. Ask them to think about how their character moves. Play "Hello, My Good Neighbor," and have the children pantomime greeting each other in character.

Next, have **Jesus** pantomime that he is teaching the crowd, and have the rest of the children be listening to him—again, in character.

Have them imagine and react to the paralyzed man being lowered down from the roof and then imagine and react to Jesus healing the man.

Finally, have the children pantomime how they would glorify God for what they had heard and what they had seen happen that day. Watch for children whose facial expressions and gestures effectively communicate their characterizations. Affirm these and use them as models for the other children.

Into the Songs

Sing "Praise to the Lord" (Short Version) From Word Clues

Bring the children back to their seats by playing "Praise to the Lord" (Short Version). Have them sing the song from the word clues on page 15.

Introduce "Praise to the Lord" (Long Version)

Explain that part of this song is also used in "Praise to the Lord" (Short Version). Have the children find it, on page 12, look through their music, and tell you why this is called the long version. (It has two additional sections—D and E.)

Sing sections A and B, and then ask them to listen to the recording of the entire song, follow the music with their fingers, and be ready to tell you if they recognize any parts of sections D and E. (The melody of section E is the same as the "Alleluia" parts of the section C, and the "Praise! O praise" part of section D is the same as section B.) Teach sections C and D.

Do Music and Motions to "A Friend Is a Wonderful Thing"

Review "A Friend Is a Wonderful Thing," and practice the motions learned last session. Then explain that motions for stanza two are as follows:

- On *big*, hold your arms out to your sides to appear big.

- On *small*, bend your knees to appear small.

- On *any old size* repeat the circling motion as before.

- Repeat the arms over shoulders motion for the four repetitions of *friend*.

- On *any time, any how, anywhere*, lower your arms and stand straight.

- On the final spoken *Friends!* return to the arms around shoulders position used before on the fermata.

Review "Hello, My Good Neighbor"

Finalize which of the children will be in Groups I and II for "Hello, My Good Neighbor." If some of the children formed pairs or clusters of characters, keep these units together in one of the two groups. If your sanctuary permits entrance to the chancel from both sides, plan for Group I to enter from the left, and Group II to enter from the right. This will allow the two groups to sing back and forth. Arrange the children in their two groups, and sing the song. Point to the groups when it is their turn to sing.

Continue Learning "Faith"

Establish which of the children will be singing the descant, and then have the children sing "Faith" twice, first from the word clues on page 15, then from memory. If the singing from memory goes well, put a blue check mark on the Songs to Learn poster in front of "Faith."

If needed, spend time during small group activities with the children singing the descant.

Small Group Activities

Conduct Line Rehearsals

Rehearse with the **Greeters** together, with the **Scribe** and the **Pharisee** together, and with the **Homeowner** and the **Storytellers** individually. Children with speaking roles should be able to deliver their lines without reading them, although they may still need prompting. (See "Rehearsing Lines," on page 41.)

Begin Staging Pantomimed Characters

Work with **Jesus**, the **Four Friends**, and the **Paralyzed Man** in the sanctuary. Indicate how and when they are to move following the stage directions in the script. Adapt these directions in advance for your setting.

Prepare Written Publicity Materials

Invite those children who enjoy writing to begin composing articles for the church newsletter or worship bulletins, informing the congregation of what they have been doing and of their upcoming presentation of *Through the Roof!*

Begin Fitting Children for Costumes

Begin fitting and assigning costumes, working with a few children at a time. Be sure to listen as the children describe their characters so that their costumes can help to express the role they are playing.

Remember that the **Jesus**, **Scribe**, **Pharisee**, and **Homeowner** silhouettes are to be clothed identically to the persons assigned those roles. (See "Costuming the Cast," on pages 44–45.)

Closing

Bring the Children Together for a Closing

Call the children together and thank them for coming. Sing "A Friend Is a Wonderful Thing," with the motions, as a closing song today. Lead them in the following prayer:

Thank you, God, for this group of people and for the exciting work you have given us to do together. Thank you for making us each special persons with important contributions to make. Be with us in the coming weeks as we prepare our gift to present to the people of this church. We pray in the name of Jesus. Amen.

Collect Name Tags

Collect the name tags and update your attendance record.

Notes

Session Seven

Preparation

Materials
- ❑ name tags
- ❑ gummed stars
- ❑ masking tape
- ❑ large sheet of paper
- ❑ paper for posters
- ❑ felt-tip markers
- ❑ old worship bulletins
- ❑ bulletin illustrations from Session Six
- ❑ house and pallet
- ❑ cassette player

Consult With Worship Planners
Meet with persons responsible for planning worship. Discuss how *Through the Roof!* will fit into the service. Give the congregation an opportunity to respond to the presentation as they usually respond to the Word proclaimed. Select hymns such as "Sing Praise to God Who Reigns Above"; "O For a Thousand Tongues to Sing"; Peter D. Smith's "When Jesus the Healer Passed Through Galilee"; Fred Pratt Green's "O Christ, the Healer"; Margaret Cropper's "Jesus' Hands Were Kind Hands"; or "Praise to the Lord, the Almighty." Write the order of worship on a large sheet of paper.

Gather Materials and Make a Sample Publicity Poster
Gather paper and felt-tip markers for the children to make posters. Make a sample poster with all necessary information.

Collect Typical Worship Bulletins
Collect an assortment of worship bulletins typical of the order of worship followed in your congregation. Place a bulletin on each child's chair.

Select Bulletin Illustration
Tally the children's choices for their favorite bulletin illustration. Consider using more than one by combining two or more illustrations or by having more than one cover.

Set Up for Rehearsal in the Sanctuary
Plan to rehearse in the sanctuary with persons chosen for speaking and pantomimed roles. Have the set and pallet ready ahead of time.

Review the Teaching Plan for Session Seven
Give special attention to the discussion of the role of *Through the Roof!* in worship.

Into the Service

Welcome the Children
Play "Praise to the Lord" (Long Version) as the children arrive. Greet them, place a 7 or a star on their name tags, and have them put their name tags on.

Start a Message Moving Through the Group
Tell the first child to arrive that you have a message to be passed through the group. Tell that child you'll whisper the message in his or her ear one time, then he or she is to pass the same instructions and this whispered message to one other person:

"The paralyzed man lowered down through the roof was forgiven and healed by Jesus."

Start Work on Posters
Show the children the sample poster you have made. Have the children create posters with pictures of scenes from the story or fancy lettering to remind people about *Through the Roof!*

Call the Group Together
Play "Praise to the Lord" (Long Version) and direct the children to their seats.

Discuss the Role of *Through the Roof!* in Worship
Announce the illustration(s) selected for the bulletin. Show the selected illustration(s) to the group. Ask the children to look at the bulletins on their chairs and suggest at what point in the worship service *Through the Roof!* could be presented. (Since *Through the Roof!* is a Bible story, it would be most appropriately presented at the time in the service when Scripture is read and the sermon is given.)

Show the children the order of worship for the service when *Through the Roof!* is to be presented. Sing one stanza of the hymn chosen to begin the service, and ask the children why they think it was chosen.

Ask the last child to receive the whispered message to repeat what he or she heard. Tell the children that this is one way to get a message to people, but it takes a long time and allows for lots of mistakes. Another way is to spend time preparing the message and bringing people together to tell them all the same thing at the same time. Indicate that what they are doing is working very hard to prepare their message, which is a gift to God and to the congregation. They are helping the congregation receive God's message.

Into the Songs

Continue Learning "Praise to the Lord" (Long Version)
Begin playing "Praise to the Lord" (Long Version), and ask the children to find the song on page 12. Sing the song together and ask the children to be ready to tell you what parts of the song they do not know. (the descant and ending of section E) Teach those parts, and practice singing the entire song from the music. Put a green check mark on the Songs to Learn poster.

Sing "Praise to the Lord" (Short Version)
If the children are able to sing "Praise to the Lord" (Short Version) from memory, put a blue check mark on the Songs to Learn poster.

Review "Hello, My Good Neighbor"
Divide the children into Groups I and II. Sing "Hello, My Good Neighbor" with the two groups singing back and forth. Practice singing the song in the rehearsal room with the children pantomiming greetings.

Review "Faith"
Have the children sing "Faith" from the word clues on page 15. If they are then able to repeat it from memory, add a blue check to the Songs to Learn poster.

Review "A Friend Is a Wonderful Thing"
Sing "A Friend Is a Wonderful Thing" through once without motions. Then divide the group into four small groups for the "arms around shoulders" motions in section B. Indicate that these groupings may change later. Repeat the song with all of the motions.

Continue Work on "Praise to the Lord" (Long Version)
Have the children turn to the word clues on page 15, and tell them that "Praise to the Lord" (Long Version) is the only song left that they haven't sung without their music. If you are using the descant in section E, assign the descant to half of the group. Sing through the descant one time, then have the descant group sing with you. Put both parts together and sing the song from the word clues. Put a brown check mark on the Songs to Learn poster.

Small Group Activities

Rehearse Persons With Speaking and Pantomimed Roles

Run through the entire script with persons assigned speaking or pantomimed roles. Hold this rehearsal in the sanctuary with the house and pallet. If lines are being memorized, those with speaking roles should need only minimal prompting.

Continue Work on Posters

Let the children continue working on the posters they started earlier.

Continue Fitting Children for Costumes

Continue fitting and assigning costumes, a few children at a time.

Closing

Bring the Children Together for a Closing

Thank the children for their good work, and tell them that during the next session they will hear and see how the whole story fits together. Let them sing a song of their choice as a closing song, and then lead them in prayer with the following words:

> *Thank you, God, for the words, the music, and the people that combine to create the gift of a story—a special story of friendship, faith, forgiveness, and healing. Prepare us for the telling, and our church for the hearing. In Jesus' name. Amen.*

Collect Name Tags

Collect the name tags and update your attendance record.

Notes

Session Eight

Preparation

Materials Needed
- ❏ name tags
- ❏ gummed stars
- ❏ masking tape
- ❏ house and pallet
- ❏ large sheet of paper
- ❏ tape
- ❏ costumes
- ❏ cassette player

Arrange for the Use of the Sanctuary

Reserve the sanctuary for the children. Move the Songs to Learn poster to the sanctuary. Set up the house and pallet.

Prepare a Sheet for the Sanctuary Activity

At the top of a large sheet of paper write "Sanctuary: A Special Place." Tape the paper in the sanctuary where you can write on it and where the children can see it.

Identify Parts Needing Attention

Make notes as to the parts of the music, narration, or movement with which the children are less confident. Plan to spend time as needed on those elements during this session.

Into the Service

Welcome the Children

Play the recording of "Hello, My Good Neighbor" as the children arrive. Greet them, place an 8 or a gummed star on their name tags, have them put their name tags on, and direct them to the sanctuary.

Explore the Sanctuary

Ask the children to think about things that make the sanctuary a special place, and then allow them to explore the sanctuary silently for a few minutes. Bring them together and ask them what things people find there to help them sense that God is with them, what things help them praise God, and what things help them feel better when they aren't feeling good.

Think Together About the Congregation

Write their ideas on the large sheet of paper headed "Sanctuary: A Special Place."

Ask the children to think about the needs of those people who will be in the congregation on the day *Through the Roof!* is presented. Let them share their responses, then tell them that as worship leaders, it will be their responsibility to help people have a good experience in worship—an experience that will meet some of their needs.

Explain that today you want to make sure that each song is polished, beautiful, and ready—red check marks on the Songs to Learn poster for each one. By the end of this session, everyone should know where each song fits in the telling of the story.

Into the Songs

Introduce the "Prelude and Greeting"

Tell the children that the drama begins with a "Prelude and Greeting." Explain that only the **Greeters** will be seen when the story begins, so you want everyone to hear the music and greeting now. Have the **Greeters** do their lines as you play the "Prelude and Greeting" music.

Work on "Hello, My Good Neighbor," Music and Movement

Review "Hello, My Good Neighbor," polishing and fixing any parts that need work. Put a red check mark on the Songs to Learn poster to indicate that the song is ready for presentation.

Divide into Groups I and II and be ready to practice entering the chancel area. When everyone is in place, ask the children to listen to what the **Homeowner** says just before they enter. Have **Jesus**, the **Scribe**, and **the Pharisee** enter as the **Homeowner** speaks, then have the crowd practice their entrance.

If the voices of the **Four Friends** and the **Paralyzed Man** are needed, they will need to exit quickly and prepare for their entrance after this song.

Do Music and Motions to "A Friend Is a Wonderful Thing"

Tell the children that they will be in and around the house for the rest of the story. When it is time to sing, they will stand, face the congregation, and sing. Have them stand, position them so that all are seen, and make sure that they are clear about the four groups for the "hands on shoulders" motions. Practice singing "A Friend Is a Wonderful Thing" with motions. Work on places where the children appear insecure. Put a red check mark on the Songs to Learn poster.

Have **Storyteller 1** tell the next part of the story as the **Four Friends** enter carrying the **Paralyzed Man**. Encourage the children in the crowd to remain focused on **Jesus**. Have the children sing "A Friend Is a Wonderful Thing" as they will do it for the presentation.

Put the Finishing Touches on "Faith"

Practice "Faith," working on any parts that need attention, then put a red check mark on the Songs to Learn poster. Ask **Storyteller 2** to tell the next part of the story as the **Four Friends** lower the pallet from the roof and the **Paralyzed Man** appears in front of **Jesus**. Have the children sing "Faith" as they will do it for the presentation.

Work on "Praise to the Lord" (Short Version)

Explain that the next part of the story is told by a **Scribe** and a **Pharisee**. Let the children hear that part of the story as **Jesus** and the **Paralyzed Man** do their pantomimes, and then sing "Praise to the Lord" (Short Version). Work on any parts of the song that need improving, and put a red check mark on the Songs to Learn poster.

Work on "Praise to the Lord" (Long Version)

Have the children sing the song first from the word clues on page 15, then sing it from memory. Put a blue check mark on the Songs to Learn poster.

Explain that the last part of the story is told by the **Homeowner** before "Praise to the Lord" (Long Version). Have the **Homeowner** tell that part of the story as the **Four Friends** and the **Paralyzed Man** make their exit, then have the children sing the song from memory. Work on any places in the song that need attention, and then put a red check mark on the Songs to Learn poster.

Note that the **Four Friends** and the **Paralyzed Man** will have to rejoin the group quickly after their exit if their voices are needed for the final song.

Small Group Activities

Complete Costume Fitting

Work with those children who have not been fitted for costumes or who need to have adjustments made. Plan to have costumes complete before the dress rehearsal during Session Nine. An extended session might be required to complete all costuming.

Work With Individuals or Groups Needing Attention

If individual characters, groups of characters, or groups of singers need some additional attention in order to polish words, music, or movement, spend time with those persons. In many cases this will involve a time commitment beyond the rehearsal hour.

Closing

Bring the Children Together for a Closing

Tell the children that the dress rehearsal during the next session will allow them to run through the story two times—just as it will be done on the day of the presentation. Let them know where to meet, what time, where to find their costumes, when to put them on, and so forth—everything they need to know in order for the rehearsal to run as smoothly as possible. Answer any questions they may have. A note to their families might prove helpful.

Thank the children for their cooperation and hard work. Sing "Faith" as a closing song, and then invite them to close their eyes. Ask them to picture themselves putting the last piece in a large jigsaw puzzle, and then pray with the following words:

> *Lord, we've spent many hours putting the pieces to this story together. Thank you for being with us as each piece has gone into place. We have one more piece to go, and then we'll be ready to tell the story to the congregation. Keep the words and the music and the movements clear in our minds. We ask this in Jesus' name. Amen.*

Collect Name Tags

Collect the name tags and update your attendance record.

Notes

Session Nine

Preparation

Materials Needed
❏ name tags
❏ gummed stars
❏ set and costumes

Prepare Set and Costumes

Put the set—including the silhouettes—in place so that everything can be rehearsed exactly as it will be done in the presentation. Arrange costumes exactly as they will be prior to the presentation.

Post the Order of Worship

Post the order of worship which you prepared for Session Seven.

Into the Service

Welcome the Children and Get Them Costumed

Greet the children, place a 9 or a gummed star on their name tags, and have them leave their name tags with you. Update attendance records and prepare a list of those children who have had the best attendance.

Direct children to the persons who are helping with costumes.

Assemble the Children in the Sanctuary

Gather the children together and review how the dress rehearsal will be conducted. Tell them that they will do a complete run-through without stopping. Ask them to hold all questions until after this first run-through. Assure them that you will then answer their questions and share the notes you've taken during the first run-through.

Explain the importance of cooperation. Seeing everything put together will be exciting for them, but you need their very best behavior and help to make everything work well.

Remind the children where in the worship service their presentation will take place by showing them the order of worship posted on the wall. Encourage them to listen carefully to the story as the characters are speaking so that they can react to what is happening in ways the story suggests. Tell them that after they have sung the closing song, they will leave their costumes on but go into the congregation and be seated until the end of the service.

Lead the Children in a Focusing Prayer

Ask the children to be very quiet, very still, and to listen to their breathing. Give yourself and the children a moment to focus, and then pray with the following words:

> *Lord, we have a story to tell. It's a very good story, and we are very good storytellers. Keep our minds clear, help us remember, and be with us as we wrap up this special gift for the people who will come to hear our story. We pray in Jesus' name. Amen.*

Do the First Run-Through

Position the children where they are to be when the "Prelude and Greeting" begins. As the story progresses, give as few directions as possible. Take notes on anything that does not flow smoothly or work well, as well as those parts or persons that deserve special praise. Try not to stop, and save all comments and suggestions for after the first run-through.

Review the First Run-Through

After the first run-through, review your notes with the children. Begin with those portions that went particularly well, and then alert them to anything needing improvement. Answer any questions the children may have, and prepare for the second run-through.

Do and Review the Second Run-Through

Have the children go to their beginning places and do a second complete run-through. Again, work toward stopping as little as possible, but feel free to stop and make corrections if there seems to be a major problem. After the second run-through, gather the children center stage and thank them for their cooperation and hard work. If you have additional notes, review them with the children quickly.

Closing

Prepare the Children for the Presentation

Acknowledge those children with the best rehearsal attendance record. Affirm once again all of the work they have put into preparing this story to tell to the congregation. Make sure they know where they are to be before the presentation and what time they are to be there. A short note to parents, particularly if your group has several younger children, would be appropriate.

Lead the Children in Prayer

Lead the children in a prayer that captures the experience that you have had together while preparing *Through the Roof!* as well as offering thanks to God for such a beautiful story of friendship and faith.

Gather Costumes

Indicate to the children where their costumes are to go. Gather the costumes and prepare them for the presentation.

Notes

Session Ten

OVERVIEW OF PRESENTATION

Preparation
Prepare the Set and Costumes
Prepare Yourself

Into the Service
Welcome the Children
Review the Songs
Pray With the Children
Direct the Children Quietly to Their Places

Preparation

Materials Needed
❏ set and costumes

Prepare the Set and Costumes
Check and double-check all of the set components and the costumes. It is very important that everything be ready and in place before the children arrive.

Prepare Yourself
Excited children need to be surrounded by calm, prepared adults. As you prepare with prayer, think through the entire story. In your mind, picture the children moving into their places, going through the narration, songs, and pantomime, then dispersing into the congregation. Picture the congregation and their eagerness to receive the children's gift of a story. Give thanks to God that you have had the opportunity to give leadership to this experience.

Into the Service

Welcome the Children
As the children arrive, calmly guide them to their places, help them into their costumes, and have them sit quietly until everyone is dressed and ready.

Review the Songs
Take a few minutes to quickly sing through each song, reminding the children of any special places that need attention.

Pray With the Children
Ask the children to bow their heads for a few minutes of silent prayer. Encourage them to think through the story, what they are to say and sing and how they are to move, and to picture themselves doing their very best. Close your prayer time with the following words:

*Our songs all are ready,
    our lines have been
        learned,
    we know when to
        move and to where.
So come now, Lord Jesus,
    your people await
    the wonderful story
        we share!*
Amen.

Direct the Children Quietly to Their Places
Lead the children quietly to their places and let the story begin!

Building the Set

Purpose of the Set
• To help the cast and congregation imagine themselves in another time and place
• To suggest the interior space of the house

Materials for the House
❑ **Portable room dividers and/or a wooden frame** to support heavy paper, cardboard, or fabric for the walls (see illustrations). A moveable room divider can be used as the center section of the house, with frames for the side walls attached to the divider.
❑ **Sheets of heavy paper** (butcher paper, brown wrapping paper, or even grocery bags cut and opened), large pieces of **cardboard**, or **heavy fabric** (canvas or unbleached muslin) to create the walls of the house
❑ **Tempera paints**—gray, brown, or reddish-brown—to create a stone, clay brick, and mortar pattern on the walls
❑ **Staples or tacks** to mount walls on frame or room divider
❑ **Paint brushes**
❑ **Clean up materials**
❑ **Table** sturdy enough for four children to stand on
❑ **Step** for children to get on table
❑ **Low stools or benches** arranged inside the house for **Jesus**, the **Scribe** and **Pharisee** to sit on.
❑ **llustrations or descriptions of Palestinian homes** from books such as *Illustrated Bible Dictionary*, General Editor Herbert Lockyer, Sr. (Thomas Nelson, 1986), pp. 494–495; *Everyday Life in New Testament Times*, by A.C. Bouquet (Charles Scribner's Sons, 1953), pp. 29–31; *The Land & People Jesus Knew*, by J. Robert Teringo (Bethany House, 1985), pp. 40–43; *The Victor Handbook of Bible Knowledge*, by V. Gilbert Beers (Victor Books, 1981), p. 353, p. 373; or *Manners and Customs of Bible Times*, by Ralph Gower (Moody Press, 1987), pp. 30–35.

Instructions to the Leader
Plan the set to fit the available space in your chancel area. Make the house wide enough to hide the movement of the **Four Friends** and the **Paralyzed Man** when they are behind it. Make the house high enough so that the heads and shoulders of the **Four Friends** are visible when they are standing on the table.

Put a concealed opening or trap door at the bottom of the backdrop to allow the paralyzed man to slip in and lie at Jesus' feet, unseen by the congregation until the appropriate moment. If you are using a room divider that extends to the floor, the trap door can be placed in a side wall, close to the center section.

Create additional floor area with portable platforms or risers as necessary.

Finalize a design and complete the basic construction prior to Session One for children to begin painting the walls.

Since the small group activity time is brief, pace the work so that the painting is completed by the end of Session Four.

Have adults (or mature youth) assist the children with painting.

As you work with the children on the set, talk to them about what homes during Jesus' time were like. Discuss how the set will help the congregation imagine where the story takes place and will help make it seem as though the **Four Friends** are actually lowering the **Paralyzed Man** through the roof.

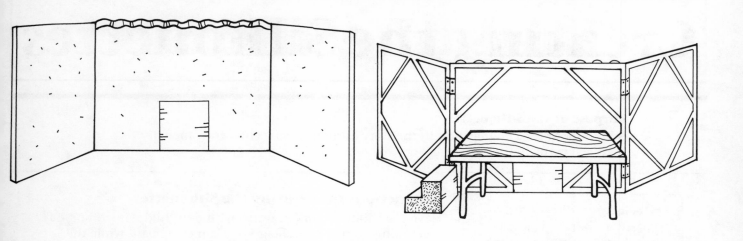

Materials for the Pallet

❏ **A heavy, dark colored blanket** (the type available in military surplus stores would work well)

❏ **Two wooden poles**, at least five feet in length and sturdy enough to support a child's weight

❏ **Two ropes**, each about three times the height of the back wall of the house

Instructions to the Leader

Plan your work so that the pallet is ready for Session Six.

Fold the sides of the blanket in toward the center and around the ropes (see illustration), making the center section about two feet wide. Stitch down both sides to create a channel.

Insert poles into the channels and your pallet is ready.

Hide the ropes underneath the **Paralyzed Man** when he is carried in. At the point in the story when the **Four Friends** carry the **Paralyzed Man** behind the house on their way to the roof, they slide the poles from the channels, fill the pallet with blankets or pillows to make it look as though the **Paralyzed Man** is inside, and draw the ropes up to make the pallet look "like a sack of grain," as **Storyteller 2** says. Stepping up onto the table, they lower the pallet slowly by the ropes.

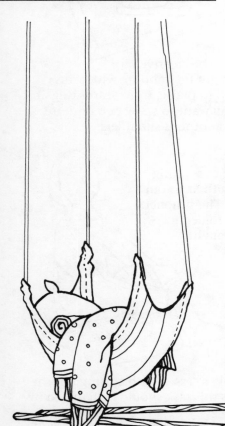

Creating the Silhouettes

Purpose of the Silhouettes
- To interest the congregation in the story as soon as they enter the sanctuary
- To create the illusion of a great crowd

Materials
- ❏ **Sheets of cardboard or foam core board** (from an art supply store) large enough to trace around a child's body
- ❏ **Utility knife**
- ❏ **Masking tape**
- ❏ **Tempera paint**—dark colors such as gray, brown, or black if the silhouettes are all to be painted in solid colors; a variety of colors if they are to be painted in biblical costume
- ❏ **Paint brushes**
- ❏ **Containers of water**
- ❏ **Clean up materials**
- ❏ **Newspapers**
- ❏ **Glue**

Instructions for Creating the Silhouettes
Have the children work in teams with one child lying on or standing against a cardboard or foam core board while the others trace around his or her body.

If all of the children are making silhouettes, encourage them to be creative with their positions. Some might be standing with arms folded, some with arms raised in praise, some leaning against the house. Some children may want to show two or more characters with arms on one another's shoulders.

In order to show a silhouette in a sitting position, have the child lie with arms out to either side and toes pointed. The silhouette, when cut out, could then be folded into a sitting position with arms brought together around the knees.

Some older children may be able to assist with cutting out the silhouettes, but in most cases this task should be handled by leaders.

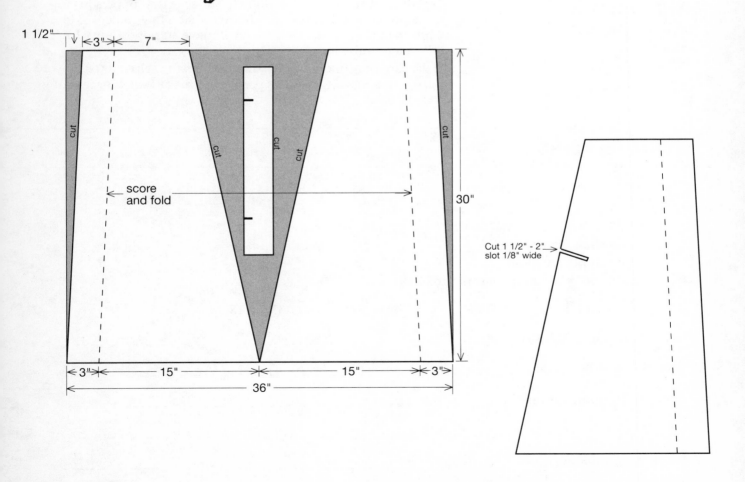

The four primary silhouettes—**Jesus**, the **Homeowner**, the **Scribe**, and the **Pharisee**—will be costumed exactly like the children playing those characters, and must have sturdy stands in order to be free-standing and support the costumes. They may be painted a solid, dark color to distinguish them from the other silhouettes if the others are to be painted in biblical dress. The other silhouettes may either be free-standing or mounted on a wall.

Pace the work so that the silhouettes are completed by the end of Session Five.

Encourage cooperation—older children helping younger children; pairs of children working together; specific children doing a particular task for everyone, such as cutting or affixing the stand.

Explain to the children that the silhouettes, when several are used, will create the impression of a great crowd. At those points in the story where interaction between the children is called for, some of them might want to treat the silhouettes as real people and interact with them as well!

As you arrange the silhouettes on the set, place the **Homeowner** silhouette upstage (toward the congregation) from the house, the **Jesus** silhouette inside the house, and the **Scribe** and **Pharisee** silhouettes across from Jesus inside the house.

1 1/2"

3" 7"

cut   cut   cut   cut   cut

score and fold

30"

3" 15" 15" 3"

36"

Cut 1 1/2" - 2" slot 1/8" wide

Holding Auditions

Purpose of the Auditions
- To identify dramatic talent and potential for worship leadership
- To select persons for speaking roles (**Greeters 1** and **2, Homeowner, Storytellers 1** and **2, Scribe,** and **Pharisee**) and for pantomimed roles (**Jesus,** the **Paralyzed Man,** and the **Four Friends**)

<table>
<tr><td>

Materials
- ❑ LEADER/ACCOMPANIST EDITION of musical
- ❑ *Singer's Edition*
- ❑ **Space** where auditions can be held privately
- ❑ **Copies of the audition guide** to be completed for each child auditioning

</td><td>

Instructions for Holding the Auditions

Familiarize yourself with the roles and have in mind the kind of personality needed for each character.

Decide prior to the auditions (Sessions Two and Three) whether the lines will be memorized or read for the presentation.

Audition children individually.

Select a passage to be used for the auditions. The **Homeowner's** first two speeches on page 48 (*Singer's Edition,* page 3) and the speech of **Storyteller 1** on page 52 (*Singer's Edition,* page 6) are two possibilities.

Create a familiar situation for determining ability to pantomime; for example, lifting a heavy object or greeting friends.

Explain that the auditions will help the selection of persons for the principle roles. Tell the children that while some will be assigned these roles, they each will have an opportunity to develop individual characters.

Make sure the children understand that being selected for one of the speaking roles requires spending time at home for learning their lines.

</td></tr>
</table>

AUDITION GUIDE

NAME _____ AGE _____ GRADE _____

1—Child shows exceptional ability
2—Child shows strength
3—Child shows potential
4—Child shows need for concentrated help

SKILLS	RATING	COMMENTS
A. Reading Ability	_____	_____
B. Vocal Projection	_____	_____
C. Dramatic Skills	_____	_____
D. Physical Expression	_____	_____
E. Confidence/Poise	_____	_____

Rehearsing Lines

Purpose of Rehearsing the Lines
- To prepare children with speaking roles to deliver their lines with clarity and confidence
- To enable the individual characters to come alive with dramatic emphasis and to tell the story well

Materials
- *Singer's Edition*
- LEADER/ACCOMPANIST EDITION
- **Space** where line rehearsals can be held without disruption

Instructions for Rehearsing the Lines

Be ready to direct line rehearsals beginning with Session Four.

Decide in advance whether lines are to be memorized or read. The ideal is memorization, although this will not be possible in every situation. If lines are read, the characters move out of the scene to the pulpit or lectern. Characters need to be very secure with the lines even if they are reading, and deliver their lines with dramatic emphasis.

Know how you want speaking parts to be delivered and work toward this end. Model for the children the mental image of the character you have in mind, but allow for their personal interpretations as well.

Talk with the children about their characters, emphasizing that development of the character is as important as learning the lines.

Explain the meanings of words and phrases so that the characters understand what they are saying.

Encourage the children to practice their lines at home, alone in front of a mirror and with another person.

Practice with live microphones, if they are to be used, prior to the dress rehearsal.

Insist during rehearsals with other characters that they listen to each speaker. Listening to the others can help them with their delivery as well.

Encourage the children to take a deep breath and focus on their characters before they speak.

Preparing Publicity

Purpose of Publicity
- To create congregational awareness, involvement, and anticipation
- To utilize *Through the Roof!* as an opportunity to draw inactive members or people from outside the church into congregational worship

Materials
- ❏ **Supplies for making posters** or other visuals (markers, paint, posterboard, tape)
- ❏ **A list of contact persons** from local newspapers, radio and television stations, with telephone numbers and addresses
- ❏ **Videotaping equipment**

Instructions for Preparing the Publicity

Plan to involve the children as much as possible in creating publicity materials.

Use the publicity to help create momentum and a sense of anticipation among the cast and the congregation.

In all publicity, emphasize that *Through the Roof!* will be presented as a proclamation of the Word during congregational worship. This is a presentation of a gift to the congregation rather than a performance.

Know the deadlines for submitting announcements to the church office for worship bulletins, newsletters, Sunday morning announcement time, and so forth.

Direct children who enjoy writing to compose newsletter or newspaper publicity articles during the Session Six small group activity time.

Have the children work on posters during the Session Seven small group activity time.

Encourage the children to invite their friends and families as a means for witnessing to others.

Consider some of the following additional strategies:

Contact your local newspaper to see if it is interested in publishing a picture of the children practicing (newspapers prefer a picture of the children actually doing something rather than standing in a line)

Have two of the children (perhaps members of the crowd) appear in character to promote *Through the Roof!* during the Sunday school or worship announcement time

Have the children paint a scene from the story and display it in the church entrance

Videotape a sixty-second commercial and play it for adult Sunday school classes, Sunday morning fellowship times, or other church gatherings

Have the children sing "Faith" as an anthem during worship a week prior to the presentation (earlier if they are prepared to do so)

Have the children design bulletin inserts announcing *Through the Roof!*

Staging the Story

Purpose of Staging
• To enable the cast to maintain the flow of the presentation with intentional, natural movement
• To position characters for the most effective delivery of songs, pantomime, and spoken lines

Materials Needed
❑ **Notebook** for staging notes
❑ **Pen or pencil**
❑ **A sketch of the space where the musical is to be staged** and several copies of the sketch for mapping out the movement.

Instructions for Staging the Story

Read through the entire script and mark each place where there is movement of individuals, groups of characters, or the entire cast.

Using the sketches of the stage area, map out entrances, positions, on-stage movements, and exits. Having this done in advance will make your rehearsals flow much more easily.

Make sure that movements do not obscure principle characters.

Work with the entire cast so that they sustain their characters at all times—even as they move from the chancel into the congregation after singing "Praise to the Lord."

Insist that the children remain attentive while they are learning staging so that their movements can be memorized.

Advise the children not to turn their backs to the congregation (unless required to do so in the story).

Have the movements and actions of **Jesus**, the **Scribe**, the **Pharisee**, the **Four Friends**, and the **Paralyzed Man** well thought out before you begin working with them during the Session Six small group activity time.

Prepare for the challenge of creating the illusion that the **Paralyzed Man** is actually being lowered from the roof. Follow the stage directions as written. A slide whistle (sound effect provided on the *Instrumental Recording*) or descending glissando on the piano adds fun to the lowering of the pallet. Be ready to work with all individual characters by Session Seven and with the entire cast by Session Eight.

Have some of the children in the crowd team up in twos or threes to pretend to be family units or groups of friends.

Encourage the older children to assist the younger ones in learning the staging.

Costuming the Cast

Purpose of Costuming the Cast
• To enable the cast members to live into their roles
• To aid in setting the story in biblical times

Materials
❑ Sheets, used draperies, fabric remnants—solid colors or striped patterns
❑ Sewing materials
❑ Illustrations or descriptions of biblical dress in Jesus' time found in reference materials such as *Biblical Costumes for Church and School*, by Virginia Wilk Elicker (A.S. Barnes and Co., 1953); *The World Into Which Jesus Came*, by Sylvia Root Tester (The Child's World, Inc., 1982), pp. 12–13; *The Land & People Jesus Knew*, by J. Robert Teringo (Bethany House, 1985), pp. 56–69; *Manners and Customs of Bible Times*, by Ralph Gower (Moody Press, 1987), pp. 12–21.

Instructions

Talk with the children about their characters before assigning or making a costume for them. Remember that each member of the cast will be portraying a specific character—either a character named in the musical or one of his or her own creation.

Check to see what costumes the church already has available.

Consult reference materials for additional information and ideas about clothing worn in Jesus' time.

Costumes will be fitted during Sessions Six, Seven, and Eight. Pace your work so that all costumes are fitted prior to the dress rehearsal, Session Nine. Schedule extra time for work on the costumes if necessary.

Keep in mind that the girls and boys need to be able to move freely in their costumes.

Children portraying adult women wear full, flowing-sleeved gowns and head veils. Wind a small turban around the head with a strip of soft material 12 to 20 inches wide and 2 yards long, and attach a veil—2 yards of soft, semisheer material—to the turban. Add a belt or sash around the waist.

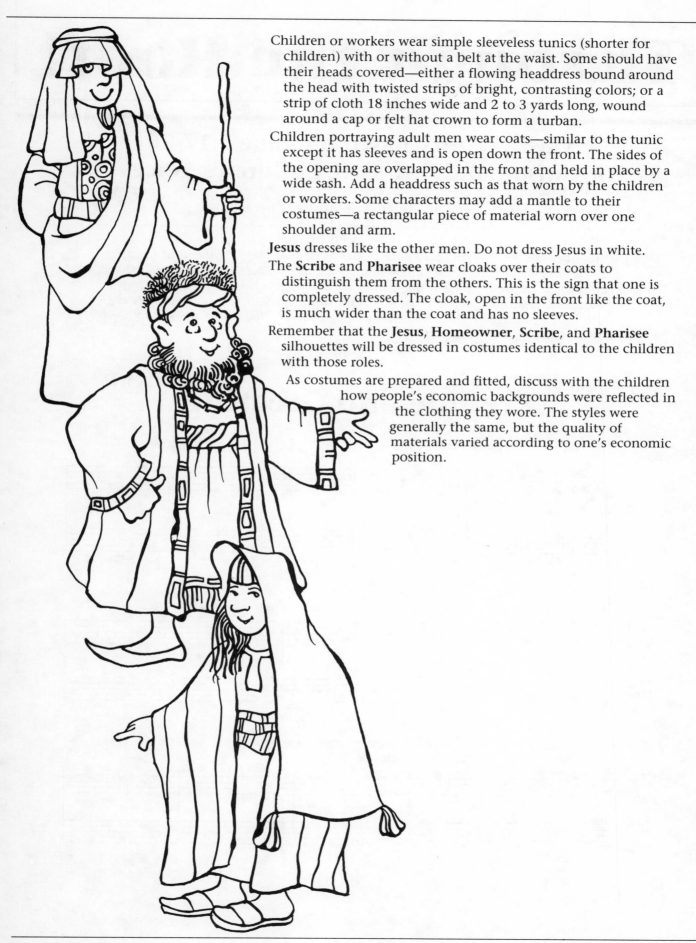

Children or workers wear simple sleeveless tunics (shorter for children) with or without a belt at the waist. Some should have their heads covered—either a flowing headdress bound around the head with twisted strips of bright, contrasting colors; or a strip of cloth 18 inches wide and 2 to 3 yards long, wound around a cap or felt hat crown to form a turban.

Children portraying adult men wear coats—similar to the tunic except it has sleeves and is open down the front. The sides of the opening are overlapped in the front and held in place by a wide sash. Add a headdress such as that worn by the children or workers. Some characters may add a mantle to their costumes—a rectangular piece of material worn over one shoulder and arm.

Jesus dresses like the other men. Do not dress Jesus in white.

The **Scribe** and **Pharisee** wear cloaks over their coats to distinguish them from the others. This is the sign that one is completely dressed. The cloak, open in the front like the coat, is much wider than the coat and has no sleeves.

Remember that the **Jesus**, **Homeowner**, **Scribe**, and **Pharisee** silhouettes will be dressed in costumes identical to the children with those roles.

As costumes are prepared and fitted, discuss with the children how people's economic backgrounds were reflected in the clothing they wore. The styles were generally the same, but the quality of materials varied according to one's economic position.

Through the Roof!

A Musical Story Based on Luke 5:17-26
For Unison and Two-Part Children's Voices

by Terry Kirkland

*(All silhouettes should be in place prior to the service. As the "Prelude and Greeting" music begins, the **Greeters** enter and stand center stage. Their words of welcome begin at the place marked (*) in the music and should be spoken in a bright, conversational manner. The lines should flow along naturally—as though only one person were speaking. The music creates a happy, welcoming atmosphere, and need not be matched to the text.)*

Prelude and Greeting

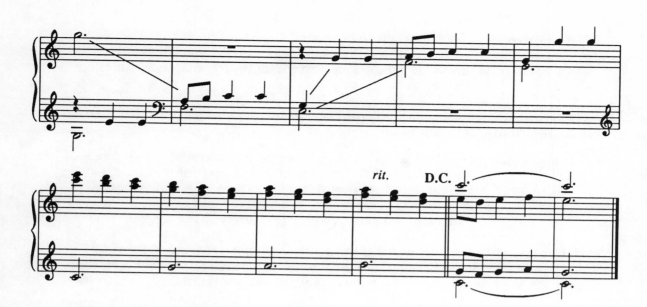

Greeter 1: A story!

Greeter 2: From the Bible!

Greeter 1: From the Gospel of Luke.

Greeter 2: Chapter 5, verses 17 through 26.

Greeter 1: It's a really good story.

Greeter 2: We call it *Through the Roof!*

Greeter 1: We're anxious to tell it.

Greeter 2: And for you to hear it.

Greeters 1 & 2: We think that you'll like it a lot!

Greeter 1: *(with a sweeping gesture toward the house)* This is the house where the story takes place.

Greeter 2: *(with a gesture toward the silhouette of the* **Homeowner***)* And this is the person who owns the house.

Greeter 1: The people inside the house are special guests.

Greeter 2: You'll hear all about them in a few moments.

Greeter 1: For now, watch and listen.

Greeter 2: Relax and enjoy.

Greeter 1: As you discover with us that friendship

Greeter 2: and faith

Greeter 1: are wonderful things!

Greeters 1 & 2: Things that sent one person *Through the Roof!*

(As the music ends, the **Greeters** *exit backstage. The* **Homeowner** *enters, moves the* **Homeowner** *silhouette into the "crowd," and turns to the congregation to begin telling the story.)*

Homeowner: Hello! Welcome to my house! Not a very grand house, as you can see; nothing special about it at all. No one would ever have given this house a second look except for the fact that Jesus came here one day.

*(While the **Homeowner** continues the story, **Jesus** enters, moves the **Jesus** silhouette into the "crowd," and sits inside the house.)*

Homeowner: Jesus had been preaching, teaching and performing wonderful miracles all over the countryside—and he chose *my* house that day! You can imagine how excited I was! No one important had ever been a guest in my house—not until the visit of Jesus. Suddenly I had important guests coming from everywhere!

*(**Scribe** and **Pharisee** enter as the **Homeowner** continues speaking. They move the **Scribe** and **Pharisee** silhouettes into the "crowd" and stand inside the house. **Jesus** greets these persons and engages them in pantomimed conversation.)*

Homeowner: Devout Jewish men called Pharisees and teachers of Jewish Law called scribes came from every village in Galilee and Judea. Some had even come from Jerusalem! My little house had never been so honored. But that's not all. News about Jesus spread quickly. The power of the Lord was with him in a special way. People were being healed! Everyone who heard about Jesus wanted to see him. So they came: friends, neighbors, farmers, shopkeepers, children with their parents—everybody!

(Music begins.)

Homeowner: And they came from everywhere!

*(The singers enter. The first to arrive go inside the house and arrange themselves around **Jesus** and the **Scribe** and **Pharisee**. The others remain outside the house. All pantomime greetings as they enter and move into place. By the end of the song, everyone should be in place, some sitting and some standing, all quietly listening to **Jesus**.)*

Hello, My Good Neighbor

Lilting and playful, in 2 (♩. = 60)

Hel - lo, my good neigh-bor, and greet - ings to you. Hello, my good neigh-bor, and how do you do? We are fine,_____ we are
well,_____ and we hope you are, too.

Hel-

* *I and II indicate divisions of two groups of children singing back and forth to each other as they enter.*

what a great day!

D

rit.   mp Slower   a tempo

Oh, what a great day!

*(The **Homeowner** moves downstage as **Storyteller 1** moves with some difficulty out of the crowd. They greet each other silently as they pass. The **Homeowner** moves into the crowd, looking for a good spot to see and hear **Jesus**. **Storyteller 1** faces the congregation and continues the story.)*

Storyteller 1: The house was so full there wasn't room for everybody. So, those of us who couldn't get in sat down on the ground outside. That was all right. We didn't mind. Jesus was there. And so were we. It was so quiet you could have heard a pin drop. Everybody wanted to hear what Jesus had to say. It *was* a great day!

*(The **Four Friends** enter from the back of the sanctuary, carrying the **Paralyzed Man** down the aisle on the pallet, walking slowly toward the house.)*

Storyteller 1: I took my eyes off of Jesus for just a moment, and noticed something strange. Four men were coming down the road carrying some sort of load. I wondered what it could be. It looked like a blanket on poles. As they came closer, I realized that I was right. It was a pallet—a thin mattress—fastened between two poles like a stretcher. There was a man on it!

*(The **Four Friends** pantomime having a difficult time getting the **Paralyzed Man** through the crowd to **Jesus**. They should attempt one way of entry and when they are unsuccessful, try another. After two or three attempts, they set the **Paralyzed Man** down and pantomime explaining to him what was happening.)*

51

Storyteller 1:   At first I couldn't figure out what they were doing. They carried the pallet up to the house and walked back and forth along the edge of the crowd. I remember watching them and thinking, *What a kind and thoughtful thing for these people to do!* No telling how far they had come. Perhaps a long way. That could be why they were late. They looked and looked for a comfortable place to lay their friend so that he could hear Jesus too. Maybe they came because they had heard that Jesus had the power of God to heal people. I looked at them, at the man on the pallet, and at the people crowding around the house—many of them my neighbors and friends. As we all listened to Jesus, I remember thinking to myself, *A friend is a wonderful thing!*

*(All singers stand to face the congregation. During the song, the **Four Friends** continue trying to find a way through the crowd. They then disappear behind the house with the **Paralyzed Man**. Unseen by the congregation, the **Paralyzed Man** gets off of the pallet and positions himself under the table and behind the trap door. The **Four Friends** remove the poles from the pallet and add pillows or blankets to suggest that the **Paralyzed Man** is still on the pallet, then pull the ropes to make a "sack" that they will lower from the roof.)*

A Friend Is a Wonderful Thing

Bright and playful, but not too fast (♩ = 126)

size at all, but a friend is a friend, is a friend, is a friend; an-y

time, an-y-how, an-y-where.

B

A friend is a won-der-ful thing to have, and a

won-der-ful thing to be. Oh, a friend is a won-der-ful

rit. *Slower* 1.

53

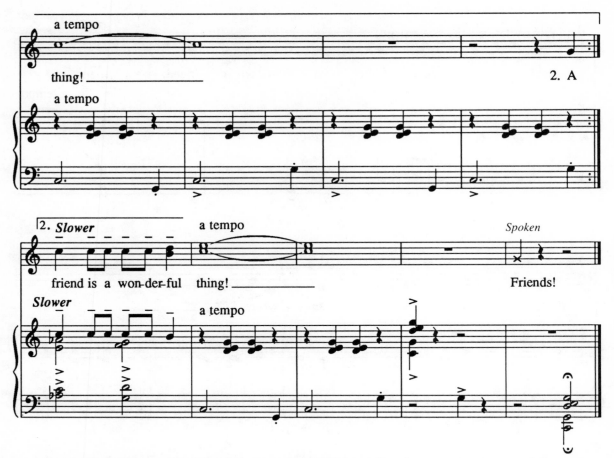

thing! _____

2. A

2. *Slower*   a tempo   *Spoken*

friend is a won-der-ful thing! _____

Friends!

(**Storyteller 1** *moves back into the crowd, and* **Storyteller 2** *moves upstage and faces the congregation to continue telling the story.*)

Storyteller 2: Everyone was listening so intently to Jesus, no one else seemed to notice the men with the pallet. I remember wondering what they were doing, but what Jesus was saying made me quickly forget about the men and the pallet. Until the noise started up on the roof. Loud noise! And dirt falling on the people below. Everyone looked up to see what was going on.

(*The* **Four Friends** *stand on the table and appear above the back wall of the house. The crowd looks up and watches the* **Four Friends** *struggle with the pallet, lift it with care over the wall, and lower it slowly by the ropes. The lowering of the pallet can be accompanied by a slide whistle or descending glissando on the piano. As the pallet reaches the floor, the crowd gathers around to obscure the movement of the* **Paralyzed Man** *as he reaches through the trap door, removes the pillows or blankets from the pallet, places them behind the house, comes through the door, and lays on the pallet.*)

Storyteller 2: I couldn't believe my eyes! The four men were lowering their friend through the roof on ropes, like a sack of grain! The pallet eased down into the middle of the crowd.

(*The crowd moves back to reveal the* **Paralyzed Man** *lying on his pallet in front of* **Jesus.***)

Storyteller 2: The next thing we knew the pallet and the man were lying on the floor right at Jesus' feet! Jesus looked down at the paralyzed man and then up at his friends on the roof. I wondered what Jesus would say to these people who had gone to such great lengths to bring this man to him. Jesus understood. It was faith that he saw in the eyes of the ones on the roof. Seeing that faith, Jesus said to the man, "Friend, your sins are forgiven you."

(Jesus reaches out his hand to the Paralyzed Man, and they freeze in that position while everyone else turns to face the congregation and sing.)

Faith

know - ing,   see - - ing in the mind;   that's the

B

faith of a child,   a   child of   God,_____ that's the faith of a

C

child   of   God._____   * For faith is the sub-stance of

things hoped for,   the ev - i - dence of things not   seen.

* from Hebrews 11:1 (King James Version)

*(Everyone returns to previous positions. The **Pharisee** and the **Scribe** move upstage, face the congregation, and continue the story, interacting as they speak.)*

Pharisee: "Your sins are forgiven you." That's what he said. I heard him. I looked around at the people there. They couldn't have understood what Jesus was saying. But I understood! I'm a Pharisee. We Pharisees know the Law. We know the Scriptures. What was Jesus teaching these people? I couldn't believe what I was hearing. Sins forgiven? That was blasphemy! Who but God can forgive sins? Did this Jesus think that he was God?

Scribe: I am a scribe—a teacher of the Law, and I was just as upset as the Pharisees were! Jesus could tell we were having a hard time with what he was saying. He looked at us the same way I look at my students when I can tell what's bothering them. "Why do you raise such questions in your hearts?" he asked. "Which is easier, to say, 'Your sins are forgiven you' or to say, 'Stand up and walk'?" Jesus said to the people, "I'm doing this so you may know that the Son of Man has authority on earth to forgive sins." Then he looked at the paralyzed man and said, "I say to you . . ."

*(**Jesus** reaches out to the **Paralyzed Man**.)*

Scribe: "Stand up and take your bed and go to your home." And he did!

*(The **Paralyzed Man** stands, gathers up the pallet, and faces **Jesus**. They freeze.)*

Praise to the Lord (Short Version)

*(At the close of the song, the **Scribe**, the **Pharisee**, and the crowd return to their positions and look in wonder at **Jesus** and the **Paralyzed Man**. The **Homeowner** moves upstage, facing the congregation to continue the story.)*

> **Homeowner:** None of us had ever seen anything like this before! We watched in awe as the men came down from the roof, worked their way through the crowd, and rejoiced with their friend as they went off down the road together.

*(The **Paralyzed Man** tries out his no-longer-paralyzed body—jumping, skipping, moving his arms and legs joyously. He is joined by the **Four Friends** who pantomime amazement as they inspect his body and then begin mirroring his actions as they praise God together and exit down the aisle toward the back of the sanctuary. The crowd watches them as they exit and then pantomime excited reactions to what has taken place, while the **Homeowner** speaks.)*

> **Homeowner:** It all happened at my house! What an exciting day! I looked at the crowd as they watched the man and his friends walking away. You should have seen their faces! They were amazed—every last one of them. They knew that God had been at work. Such strange things we saw that day! Strange and wonderful things. One other thought ran through my mind as the crowd began to leave: *Who's going to fix my roof?*

*(Singers face the congregation to sing. If the voices of the **Paralyzed Man** and the **Four Friends** are needed for the final song, have them quickly return to the group by way of a side aisle.)*

Praise to the Lord (Long Version)

Praise with the sound of the strings.   O praise,   praise,

praise to the Lord, for the Lord has done won-der-ful   things. _____

Al-le-lu – ia! Al-le-lu – ia! Al-le-lu – ia! Sing

praise_ to   the Lord! _____

(The cast disperses into the congregation for the remainder of the worship service.)